CONNECTED RAMBLINGS
OF A
LAKELAND POET

CIEL

For permissions or enquiries, please contact:

cielpoetry@yahoo.com

For more information on the author
and the energetic centre
that is his inspiration...

www.lightfromthecentre.co.uk

MIX
Paper | Supporting responsible forestry
FSC® C014138
FSC www.fsc.org

ABOVE THIRLMERE
— HEATHER JAMES

INTRODUCTION

Welcome to my first collection of poetry. I very much hope you enjoy it. Writing poetry entered my life in the spring of 2024, at the age of 46. Before then I had not written a single poem. Since when I have written many hundreds. The catalyst that initiated this awakening was a traumatic brain haemorrhage two weeks after my first Covid vaccination in May 2021 which was very challenging to recover from. A 'just sitting' meditation practice formed the cornerstone of this rehabilitation as well as plenty of time out in nature in the beautiful northern Lake District in the UK where I am very lucky to live and have historically enjoyed an active life, with my main hobby being fell running.

This self reflection time and developing a connect to my heart and breath awareness is what allowed me to heal, not just from the brain haemorrhage but also the deeper trauma and behavioural patterns that had been influencing my life historically. I had to change to be able to cope with the enforced solitude the haemorrhage brought, the slower pace of life and the acceptance that there were things I could no longer do. Now four years later, I am thankfully fully better with a vastly reframed outlook on life and a host of new skills to keep me grounded, grateful, kind and connected.

None of this, of course, would have been possible without the people in my life who have stood by and supported me along the way. Firstly Juno, my wife, whose world was thrown upside down, who had to cope whilst I was ill and did so so magnificently. There were many very challenging times particularly at home. In the early days after the haemorrhage it was severe sensitivity to light, sound, sudden or rapid movement around me. So being around our gorgeous three young children was especially difficult. I got very low sometimes. Then when I interacted too much my brain got horribly neuro-overloaded and I would have a sudden complete meltdown which was very scary for those around me, virtually always Juno and our children.

As I gradually got better this erratic behaviour still came out when my brain got fatigued, usually in the afternoon, or if I had had a poor night's sleep. But despite this, there was considerable hope. I was experiencing much greater self awareness thanks to the meditation practice and time in nature. My job role changed. My outlook changed. Humility was seared into my mainframe. I had properly learned to trust people but also to read people. Becoming self-aware at the deepest level, aware of your breath, your conduct, your values, your ethics, your thinking patterns allows you to read situations effectively in an instant.

It allows you to be more effective at your job, to be more patient and also much more creative. Creativity arrived into my life in the form of writing poetry three years after my brain bleed. The best place for creativity to thrive is a still mind. A still mind comes from being breath aware.

So thank you Juno and all the many other people close to me that stepped up when I was ill. Most notably at work Nico Chieze, Richard Swale and Debbie Slater AKA my guardian angel. Also Harriet, Chris and Justin on the farm and my sister Marie-Louisa though of course there are many more. Thank you for allowing me the time to get better by keeping our family businesses going.

Also thank you to the NHS, to the people I met on retreat who taught me to meditate and opened my eyes to the practice of kindness. There are many people in the world that operate in a community minded, selfless way who are here to help. I learned this properly through getting ill. To give and to support and help others. I have now joined their ranks and it is a wonderfully rewarding way to be. And that is why I have decided to embark on the rather scary new path to publish the poetry that flows through my hand, in the hope that it will help those that read it find inner strength and peace. To know that connecting to and looking for the best in each other is important.

The purpose of publishing this poetry is not to make money. The profits of this venture will be channelled into our newly formed charity, CIEL Rehabilitation, whose function will be to help people mentally heal in nature, through providing support to functional and creative occupational therapy providers and instilling the benefits of breath awareness and regular meditation.

I myself have a Zen practice. These poems come from in the Zen tradition what is called an awakened mind. It is a mind that has let go completely of fear and separation, and a heart and body that has awoken to love and connection. It is something that can happen to anybody. It shows us that the world we live in is deeply interconnected in so many ways that are not immediately obvious to a busy or traumatised thinking mind.

This connection, if you allow it, can guide your life and inform your life choices. It won't trip you up. You can trust it. I do. It allows you to develop deep connections with those around you, it strengthens friendships and your appreciation and reverence for the natural world and nature. It allows you to be fully present. It allows you to express your own unique creativity, to fully be with the world around you and become an inter-connected part of it in a fully conscious way.

This heart connection also neutralises external gratification as you go about your day with love and gratitude radiating from your heart. Nothing external can trump this. Simply what your body needs to be healthy and nourished is all you still have need for.

This heart connection also gives you clarity with your job and life purpose. I now have a clear understanding of my life purpose. For now this is to provide places for people to come to in the northern Lake District, both recreationally and to stay, to benefit from the stunning natural beauty our region offers. To give their minds space from their busy lives, to help see their purpose more clearly. Publishing the poems that flow through me complements this, giving people a window into a mind awakened to the beauty, simplicity, creativity and clarity of just being.

Finally, I would like to thank all those that have encouraged me to put my poetry out for public access and then to those that that have assisted in getting it to print. Namely Heather James both for her exquisite art that helps connect the book and her digital capabilities, Stuart Clarke, Stuart Beveridge for his design work bringing the book to life and Simon Hodson at Latitude Press.

I will leave you with a lovely quote from Charles Dickens that another person that merits a special mention recently brought to my attention. Julia Stanton - thank you.

"A loving heart is the truest wisdom"

ROSSET PIKE AND ROSSET CRAG
— HEATHER JAMES

This is an art, this mystic poetry
bitter pills of life taken
absorbed and reshaped, simply be
start walking towards, unshaken
the truth of its source, peace
an unfettered freedom, release

and find the forest of your dreams
where life abounds, where it teams
the wings of life they lift you up
to follow the trail to the grail cup

where those bitter pills that once were
fall apart, in an instant blur
a field of flowers dancing free
walking, sensing, a life to be

settling into the rhythms of this earth
caught in the moment, another re-birth
into the world that will never die
into the music swirling in the sky

so when you need me, I am here
these words a door, away from fear
into the light, where we always are
deep inside, that shimmering star

lustrous, powerful, true and free
the essence of you, the essence of me
the never ending world to catch and keep
the source of all, that all souls seek

Fall into the sky and become
the music of the wind
it sings the song of forever
it sings the song of limbs

dancing in the breeze
they fall about and laugh
the heron floats with ease
cascading rapids into the dark

the grey sky filling the world
as biting cold waters my eyes
the wind taking away these pearls
back to the earth, into the skies

where the wind lives, where we
are torrents of music sweet
resting in the moment, listening
to the wind, listening to the beat

Topping out into the sun
there she was alive, ablaze
the light reached, we become
a flowing force, happy days
the tops majestic crowned with snow
we skip along, little do we know

of what Blencathra used to be
to those people of our past
what it is now to you and me
a playground in the sun, a fast blast
down into the fog off the tops
legs burning, but soon it stops

all too soon dare I say
but again we will to a different tune
today she was kind, she let us play
next time slower but always boom
she hits us hard with what she is
a mighty mountain, impossible to miss

always to revere, always to admire
to climb her top like a spire
a pilgrimage up, a sacred place
her energy powerful, full of grace
never to be underestimated, that would be remiss
treat her with respect, she will give you bliss

The shimmering stars behind my eyes
as I awake into this world
the light dawning into the skies
as the world it is unfurled

may I keep you stars, within me
as I go about my day
may I see the stars within ye
as light illuminates the way

pleasure less, the moment when
the light within is lost
happiness, the moment when
the sunrise dances across the frost

the mind withdraws, the soul does find
the beauty, the pleasure of human kind
the touch in me, the touch in you
the gaiety of the world anew

held together by a hidden force
quiet, resplendent, a peaceful course
setting off the stars inside
to catch, to connect, to set aside

so burn true ye stars
that are within me
may ye burn bright, alive
for all to see

(pass something on to a succession of others)

Unborn children yet to come
where dost thou abide
unborn children of this world
floating free, may we collide

to touch, to connect
to bring about change
to touch, to protect
the wonders of this age

I call you loud
know you are divine
up in those clouds
know and you shall find

your true essence
your true light
I call to you
from beyond your sight

A beacon
to those living
and to those unborn

thoughts shawn
hearts warm
living within the thorn

The billowing clouds
the greys, light, bright
float through the day
and all through the night

wherever you are
look up to the sky
and see the clouds
from behind your eye

be in the moment with
the birds and the trees
following the light
following the breeze

Swimming in the source
swimming in the lake of jewels
snowdrops line the shore
the biting cold — never cruel

the invigorating presence of mind
the invigorating draw of here
floating in the ocean
where all abounds — we hear

the call of the dove, faint
but unmistakable never the less
the call of love, clear
that sweet enveloping caress

Ask yourself this simple question...
why be in the present moment?

if you want me to elaborate
I will say this...

the mindful breath in here –
unity with all existence
it's your choice how long you
want it to last – persistence

a temporary enlightenment, a moment
of clarity, a feeling of aah...
a deeper enlightenment, a seeing
with clarity, driving your car

days, weeks, months, years of
this deep connection
the reality of cause and effect
laid bare, no perplexion

intelligent choices, the seeing
of truth, free from fear
the energy of all existence
around you, always near

the deepest connection to life
that anyone can know
joy, compassion, strength
creativity, benevolence all grow

this is the garden of eden
this is the here and now
free from sin, free from desire
the deepest bliss in the simple – wow

The magic is in there
your hands as well
all to be done is to
empty out the shell

smack it about, that
bitch of a mind
smack it about, get
drunk and be kind

drunk on the elixir
the elixir of life
time to switch off
a mind running rife

what's to be gained
in not living true
to the gifts deep within you
to being in tune with the hue

the hue of the world
full of change and ordeal
but what's to fear
when heaven is revealed

The rain it peppered the window pane
the wind howled in the dark of night
I get up and kindle the fire
I get up and welcome my sight

the eternal mystery beyond us
grants us these days
no matter the present conditions
we are how it displays

at this precise present moment
the magick it is revealed
our mind is still and open
an abundant, fertile field

I am a man of this place
I am a man of this time
I tend to my jobs with gratitude
in the moment with the sublime

whatever the weather it does
it is the reality of the time
I embrace the rain, I embrace the cold
I am this rain, I am this rhyme

I am everything, I am nothing
I am the essence of your soul
may you sense me in the moment
may you sense me and be whole

The circle of the worlds open
soil is scattered everywhere
settling on mountains, forests
and plains — where are you?

the circle of our world is complete
the ocean is endless
fed by streams and rivers
what is you course?

the energy of the earth
alive deep within its core
yours — a mirror of ore
may you know your source

Having ceased to bring pain
I only bring joy
a state of mind to engage
to mindfully deploy

a code of conduct to keep
to illuminate the day
a code of conduct to keep
in all utterances I say

feel the whip of the wind
feel the sting of the rain
feel the energy flowing
be like a steam train

a fully stoked fire
I may be covered in soot
but I am happy, happy, whole
from head to foot

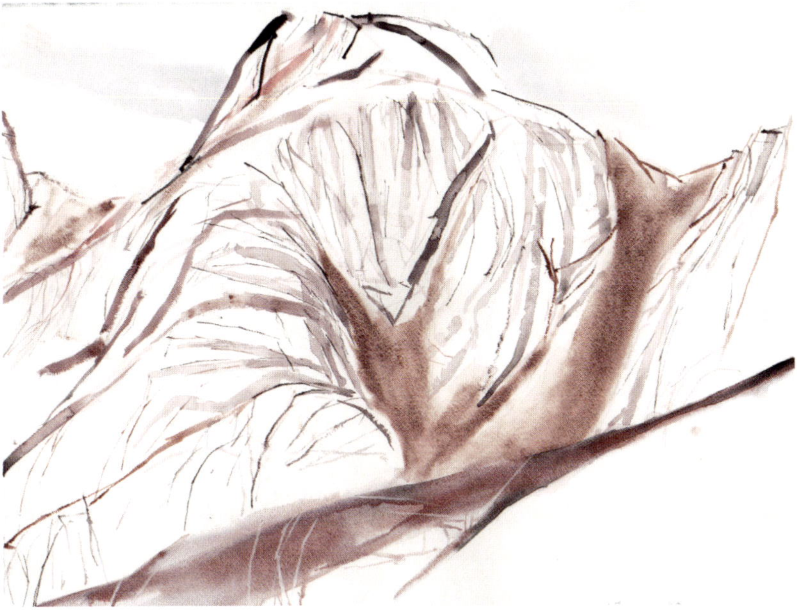

SCAFELL PIKE
— HEATHER JAMES

Now back to the mountains
and this time Scafell
deep in my consciousness
the highest to dwell

not Skiddaw or Helvellyn
or even Bow Fell
make it this high
this story to tell

sometimes approached fast
and sometimes approached slow
the Pike it is the top
visited by many but few know

the lore of this mountain
the story of the past
when the ancients visited here
to collect tools for their masts

this mountain has always given
of its stone and its life
to build others up, to point
the way out of strife

take to the high ground
take to the pure air
come play in my playground
come climb my stair

I am always here
I always have been
since man has ever existed
come taste my cream

come sharpen your tools
come sharpen your mind
come see the sunrise
seek and ye shall find

the hidden parts of my being
furthest up in the sky
the hidden parts of my being
closest to when you die

I am hard and unforgiving
you must be fully prepared
my axe I wield with impunity
at any moment you might be scared

Broad Stand my show stopper
when on your grand route
descending down to Fox's Gully
fast in clag, hard to compute

show me respect, be aware
I am king of this land
come join the ranks of those
that have prospered from my hand

I give of my energy pure
the clouds around me soar
come taste my elixir
come walk through my door

whatever of me you take home
will be etched in your soul
whether or not you come back
I am your North Pole

⟶

an elevation unsurpassed
in this country so green
an elevation unsurpassed
that many have seen

my ancestors came here
I know in my bones
they were given of this energy
to use in their homes

and now I come back
in a different time
my children will too
to experience the sublime

Scafell Pike I bless you
I thank you for your gift
Scafell Pike, I honour you
the magic in you I lift

He strode across the
ridge of knives
relaxed, accomplished
inside I cried

how could he do it
how could he glide
across that precipice
fear left aside

when I went next
we retreated with respect
ice everywhere, sky bright
a perfect reflect

I am not Chris Bonnington
I have a different mind
an amateur on the high lines
a natural with my rhymes

I run up Blencathra regularly
looking over Sharp Edge
my senses overtaken by
the changing light, my pledge

to bring these places to life
in words that do bewitch
the intoxicating energy of
places where we glitch

that bring us into nature
some more arresting than others
exposure at its extreme
Sharp Edge — it entirely smothers

→

dark thoughts, thoughts of why
it brings us into now
it brings us into contact
with the life inside us — wow!

so, whatever your comfort zone
the high places near home
they are a place to reflect
they are a place to atone

space to find the majesty
of a world beyond our mind
the call of the mountains
the call of our time

The pinks in the sky
a dazzling sight
crowding outdoors
to catch the light

spirits high after
a day somewhat mixed
a convivial dinner
the energy fixed

oh I love them so
my dear family
kind and carefree
full of artistry

all drawing the juice
from what we find
the magic in nature
connecting our kind

I look up to the sun above
I look into the light it holds
I let go of thought and become
the light itself as it unfolds

the waves of grace
dancing true
the morning light
the morning dew

the brisk bright air
playing in the trees
washing my face
washing my leaves

that within me, the
light now become
which sees all souls
which sees the young

the beauty of creation
which it reveals
it is this beauty
which our mind heals

all is contained
within this truth
beauty eternal
written on the hoof

→

an instant flash
before my eyes
the light itself
for humanity cries

oh this world
created for us
manifesting in form
but oblivious

caught in the trap
to help us evolve
those beyond it
the riddle solved

creating beauty
in forms new
to match the beauty
of the morning dew

to help others
realise this truth
sisters and brothers
under one roof

where beauty exists
where beauty thrives
where peace abounds
where dukkha dies
(dissatisfaction)

Appreciating the beauty
in every little thing
the purpose of existence
oh hear me sing

we are here on earth
with our eyes
to witness the skies
to forget the lies

to forget the vengeance
to forget the greed
to see the beauty
in the growing seed

spring has sprung
on this February day
the air warm
the atmosphere gay

the simple life
out in the garden
with the birds
our ethics harden

to be rock solid
solid as a rock
to carry our load
disharmony to block

unrelentingly positive
our minds at peace
hard as nails
a warrior fleece

The sky is ablaze
the sun is low
temporary beauty
within the flow

transient times, lines
cracks in the light
soon to be gone
as we enter the night

artistry that captures
this realised aesthetic
impermanent, illuminated
some call prophetic

simply in tune, the way
Zen practitioners at play
honing their craft
emptiness, freedom displayed

I stole a look through the trees
and saw them dancing in the breeze
playing, swaying in tune to the flow
of the lakeshore edge, the sky aglow
now here in the quiet, my mind ablaze
I remember those most special of days

can you feel the energy bright
of those pale yellow petals living true
their roots holding on with all their might
delicate, resilient, the chosen few
that persist there in the sliding sleet
where soon will flourish meadowsweet

and now in the early spring this flower
the music of which lifts our soul
captivates my mind hour by hour
its bright cheery yellow fills the hole
of wanton winter, its austere hues
along the lake with its awesome views

and so when I close my eyes at home
all around me my senses are of daffodil
I am transported to their stately throne
there by the lake in the waters still
bobbing, nodding, welcoming spring
with all the wonders it does bring

oh daffodils, you do entrance me
I am now hard-wired to your poetry
I see your colour, I see your stems
I see the world through your lens
tentative, then bold, then bright and free
the eternal image of true gaiety

Fragile beauty
changing light
the touch in me
ever so slight

I am in you
I am out there
when we connect
thoughts are spare

oh to be here
up on the hill
oh to be here
where all is still

Who is there out there
who has awoken like me
and expresses emptiness
in beautiful artistry

who hears the birds sing
not just with their ears
who is a mirror to life
without any smears

I understand that nature
always fills a gap
the gift released in me
fell through that crack

the gap in my mind
once I opened the door
and saw the bright light
no thoughts of more

creativity is infinite
in this empty spacious state
whatever then comes
truthful wisdom on a plate

so I call to all life
I call to all existence
come find me in the light
peaceful, creative persistence

LOOKING WEST FROM ABOVE WINDERMERE
— HEATHER JAMES

The clouds skit across
the morning sky
the cirrus lit up
way up high

my soul lifts up
to join the bright
oh sunrise, thou that
banishes the night

the limbs of trees
without their leaves
bow and brace
with gentle ease

the patter of rain
a trickle in the gutter
the sun is coming
my heart a flutter

a day of rainbows
is heralded this morn
creeping spring
greets us this dawn

the birds a chatter
the crocuses out
my mind is still
as I cast about

What's the point in everybody
commenting on misery
I choose not to, I choose
changing the chemistry

lifting souls up with
sweet artistry
setting minds on fire
with images of glee

look at the world
full of diversity
life thriving, flourishing
against adversity

evolution has brought us
to the place we are
the lifeless world of
its beginnings, distant, far

where we are going
we can not know
so appreciate here now
and feel the glow

of life pumping
through your veins
of being peaceful
present in the rains

that fall on this earth
to nourish our plants
that fall on this earth
as we advance

onwards, forwards
relentlessly positive
one day, all of us
will learn to forgive

Art is beauty
beauty is truth
elegant solutions
peacefully aloof

the world is alive
our bodies will die
I see my soul
up in the sky

when this life ends
there is nothing to fear
life lives on
close and near

the merit gained
in this life lived
onwards momentum
onwards sieved

until every grain
is pure and true
and we see the world
in a different hue

where beauty reins
where beauty creates
an infinite gallery
an infinite state

Less is more
the Zen way free
to simply express
raw creativity

Man is a mountain
the earth our soul
we meet in the middle
to create new life

may our souls spark
and be as one
may our light inside
connect with the sun

the emptiness of space
may it interlace
with our mind's eye
a feeling of grace

to give to our children
the values of now
the values of forever
our prize cow

The bronze tone
of this throne
sitting on the hill
once a home

the skylarks rise
as they do
showing the way
an ancient crew

transporting us to
a sacred place
the blue sky clear
without a trace

feel my words
as they interlace
into your soul
a sweet embrace

as the skylarks are
to our mind
as the sky is clear
in our kind

to see the beauty
to see the now
to be in heaven
up here. Tao.

Divine communion
this sweet poetry
divine illumination
this energy to be

infused, entwined
into the fabric of life
a still mind, empty
cuts through like a knife

into the world that is
behind the everyday
a beauty transfixing
about us displayed

for us to capture
in which to play
as the sun shines
for us to display

a mirror to truth
a mirror to beauty
a mirror to reflect
humble, never snooty

Surrender to the energy of everything
surrender to the wisdom from the sky
surrender to the light that never dies

our brain is a port
for creativity and ingenuity to arrive
for our kind to progress and thrive

it is not our place to know
it is simply our job to sow
the seeds of life and grow

Hear the birdsong loud
see with piercing sight
recurring thoughts — a cloud
equivalent to the night

(the way of all things
then obscured...)

natural order must reign
your mind to be cured

— ALIGNMENT —

A still dark night
the planets align
lit up from afar
in our time

out in space
far away from here
they orbit slowly
those silent spheres

dancing in tune
their energy strong
connections made
within the throng

now seen true
with our eyes
we come to you
up in the skies

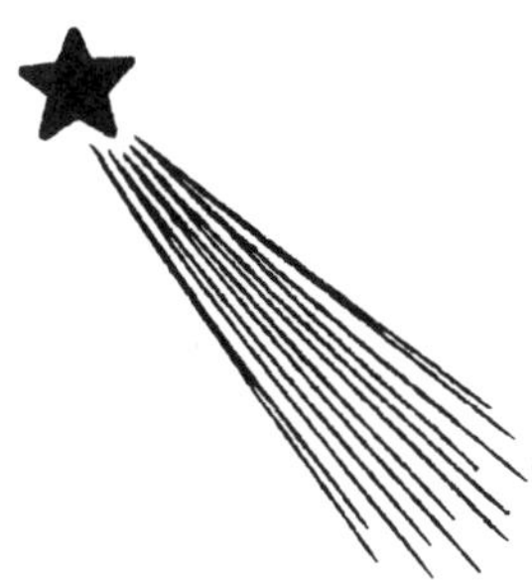

Our safety net is faith
our safety net is Samadhi
walk into the night
willingly and gladly

adapt on the spot
no fixed direction
when the wind comes
we are its reflection

we listen in tune
to the rhythm, the beat
of our own heart
where our maker we meet

Epiphany after epiphany
these poems ring true
helping people find
the One true view

once it is made and
the connection is known
all becomes peaceful
the timeless throne

the feelings of bliss
the shattering of mine
all becomes One
pure and benign

heaven on earth
right here in the now
heaven on earth
no matter the row

no matter the time
no matter the place
kindness and strength
a flow of grace

the essence in us all
once we let go and trust
whatever your faith
peace obliterates lust

peace obliterates greed
peace obliterates thought
peace obliterates all
that you were ever taught

all you need to know
comes from within
the universe inside you
may you hear me sing

The song it played
across the fell
the skylarks loud
from ground they swell

all around me still
as the orange hues
cast under the clouds
my legs unamused

the stones they sit
soaking it up
I drink it in
I drink from the cup

I slow right down
not a time to go fast
I honour this moment
in the passage vast

SAT 1 MAR 25

BOW FELL
— HEATHER JAMES

The soft hues
within the stream
our river flows
as if a dream

the hard granite
of our mind
our ethics pure
unity, refined

(come home...)

Think of me as a
bird with a stick
I build these poems
brick by brick

building then lining
a comfortable nest
in which your mind
can find its rest

to live true to your gift
always kind and aware
eyes ablaze, seeing
beauty everywhere

When you look in the mirror
what do you truthfully see
do you see beauty and
radiance and tranquillity

if you don't then you have
work to do on your soul
until you are pure
until you are whole

we see all the cracks
your reflection is clear
your aura radiates out
far and near

but the cracks are okay
they're where the light gets in
we've all got them, its
just a case of filling them in

I opened my eyes
the spears of light
dancing across the
fell that night

Arthur's Pike
awoken of old
I wrapped up
against the cold

the love in the stones
the call of the cairn
alluring, captivating
since I was a bairn

I lit my fire
paid my respects
sat under the stars
sat under the moon

I saw the stars
speak to me
I saw my ancestors
my heart did swoon

this folklore hero
Arthur was here
a man to remember
a place to revere

→

the experiences come
I feel him inside
an unstoppable force
the power of the tide

to bring peace to hand
the sharp spear of truth
the embodiment of lore
awoken, foolproof

Arthur is in us all
he is the hand of God
the code, the quests
the path to trod

The soft hues
within the stream
our river flows
as if a dream

the stone dissolves
our mind is a tool
only a fool
allows it to rule

(come home...)

For Roshi x

I walk out into the spring light
overstimulated, somewhat fraught
a whirling mass of thought
the song in me is caught

I hear the birds, attention!
my heart fills with love
the sweetest notes of nature
the softest velvet glove

the garden birds, the skylarks
the linnet or the curlew
I can not choose my favourite
they all clear my near view

the fire inside ablaze
I linger, I amaze
my mind now in harmony
I thank these special days

when the light draws long
and the bird chatter explodes
twigs carried everywhere
in tune, I write this ode

energised, hypnotised
the song draws me far
my wings open wide
the bird inside the jar

→

reaching for the light
the story of our time
fighting for our life
we wrestle away our mind

to the bird inside this jar
I hear you loud this spring
you have been calling and calling
now it is your turn to sing

sing your sweet spring song
sing for all to hear
your cage was my own making
now the sides are clear

just an empty space to fill
with your joyful presence
thank you for showing me grace
I bless your golden essence

I am spinning, I sing loud
this song of spring

My window is open, calling with
the birds, feasting on the light
I fly away into the spring air
turning cartwheels in the sky
I am high, I am drunk...

Do you know this feeling?
Letting go into the bosom of
life's abundance so utterly...
Love, the purest of all tonics
living between us and the stars
gifted by the light of all life

Our whirling spirals touching
merging, shattering our separateness

In love our hearts break open
the energy in our chests taking
over our senses
thought relegated to the ashes
of this burning heat

In the heart of the fire of
emptiness there is a fountain
of love pouring over all life. Stop
your clock. Fall into the spring
fountain, it is the sweetest of all

I am sprung, the scales have
tipped and I am here, running
wild and carefree through the
aching limbs of winter

The rush of sap into young buds
the comely purring of that once
icy stare. But beware...

Unabounded giddiness is my domain
you have a job to do heralding my train
call out loud to all that can hear
call your call of spring and work
that purpose into your heart

That swells as my train runs
                                        through your fields
that carries you as I am revealed

— — — — — — — — — — — — — —

Once I am with you
what is left of me is gone
I open my eyes in the morning
hearing your chorus song

I do your bidding
merging with your tune
with blossom on my back
I enter the room

Let me be your will
take me to the places
we are to go together
in this lifetime.

this freedom...

to follow the currents
of this reverence
to rise above the
clouds without defence

to join the sunrise
I beat this drum
the bliss of love
that all become

The bliss of love
breathing, chest heaving
breaking open, shattering
into you, our Beloved

agony, pure ecstasy
I am long gone
I care not for anything
but your song

sleep, wait your turn
this spring energy
this welling of life
it is the remedy

we have all waited
patiently all winter
for these precious moments
for life to splinter

into a billion showers
of seeds borne far
into swelling wombs
waiting for their star

what are you love
other than life itself
raw unbridled beauty
rampaging through our hearts

Emptiness is energy, light, love
creativity, spontaneity, wisdom
it is the swept away state
free of attachment and condition

raw, pure consciousness left
wielding its gift with freedom

Be that gift. Be grace.
Be compassion. Be a clear
lens to truth. Be free.

Like a bird flying through
heaven, its wings ablaze
for all to see

People only do selfish things when
they are not connected to our source
this sense of separateness is utterly
absurd and a lonely course

it is born out of inherited trauma
and conditioning in our childhood
attachments in the material world and
a lack of initiation into spirituality

the practice is simply to wake up
connect to the energy of everything
and walk through life in peace
helping others to see this reality

WINDERMERE FROM GHYLL HEAD
— HEATHER JAMES

I am the fountain of spring
feel my pulse enter your soul
let go of your suffering
feel my energy it is your pole

I stamp my staff, bare earth
this season's nourishing role
life blossoms, a re-birth
look around you and be whole

my fountain flows and flows
my sweet fragrances are coming
building into rivers of rose
hungry, you come, running

Why did this happen to me
where was so called God
my delicate fragile tree
struck through – a lightening rod

where did it come from
why triangulate on me
this delicate fruiting flower
full of vim and positivity

the weather acts mysteriously
we can only guess its ways
but whatever comes at us
that doesn't kill us — amaze

it is part of our way
to find strength deep within
to meet adversity with bravery
to help to vanquish sin

to find out who we are
to triumph and grow strong
from roots that are supported
by an innumerate caring throng

there is method in the madness
your soul is part of a tree
this has helped you find it
now rejoice and be free

our bodies are only temporary
our mind it can be a curse
our soul it is our essence
this life no dress-rehearse

Who is this seer in me
I am here at the door
don't ask for more

when you see me looking
you are not afraid
I am the knife, the blade

I write replies to what I see
that is me
an unobscured lens crafting
sweet poetry

resilient, patient, loving
and care-free
come listen to my verse
countering adversity

Throw open your blinds!
call me loud and I will hear your cry
I am your jewel sparkling in the sky

we are lovers merging in the moment
I am the pure white blossom of
the Blackthorn

you are my eyes — together we
make this beauty which can not
be torn

nothing can help you but which is
created from this thorn. The loss
and then the finding. In you I
am then re-born

feel my tenderness in your heart
and make this the day to start

go about your day with our love
in your soul. Ride my waves of
grace in your little boat

the buoyancy of spring — afloat

"For everything that is really great and
inspiring is created by the individual
who can labour in freedom"

—

Albert Einstein

"In every ability there is an ingredient which
cannot be resolved into information.
And in some skills this may be the greater
part of the knowledge required"

—

Philosopher, Michael Oakeshott

Do you hear your heart
in the smoking winds
of life's fire

—

CIEL

How can you know
what is beyond your mind
without stilling it completely
repeatedly, daily — no grind

awareness grows of an energy
which gifts us all sorts
whatever your endeavour
stillness is your port

to build ideas and your craft
to find your own creative raft
so sail across the emptiness and find
beauty, simplicity and mind refined

to be present and aware, afloat
the wave of energy that is your boat
dancing and playing throughout existence
jump into emptiness, divine persistence

The cat comes quietly
slinking past
I am in the city
huge and vast

people lost in a
world of greed
short fuses, envy
energies to read

the cat slinks on
not lost, but aware
awareness adapted
carrying urban flair

the blue sky, the birds
the green open space
they are here as well
a matrix, not a race

whatever you are
it is this to know
don't worry about others
slow down and row

row your boat
into the light
peaceful, clear
quiet yet bright

What is this twitch
this nervous energy
it is the weaver working
through your chemistry

threads of gold
dark threads of ill
come with my love
come with my chill

know me now
the ocean decides
your job is simply
my wave to ride

with gratitude, grand
with gratitude, soar
soar like a bird
no matter the chore

settle right in
channel your twitch
so the energy flows
flick the switch

THE LANGDALES
— HEATHER JAMES

The sky is clear
the sun is low
all around is still
spring aglow

up I rise
with the peace
with the sky
an enveloping fleece

There is a way
a way of grace
a force in nature
a force in space

my job is to show
how it works
how it is revealed
and its perks

change is coming
change is real
make your mind
hard as steel

ethics pure
job to serve
still mind, sharp
flow un-nerved

to help the world
on its path
to help humanity
live and laugh

its perk is peace
an inner fire
energy when needed
humility, our spire

The cobwebs blown off
I call to the sun
come refract through me
and amethyst become

a child of February
I glisten and dazzle
still and at large
indifferent to hassle

I choose a place
where I can energise
as I watch my son
jump into the skies

helped by the power
that flows through us all
a family connected
to the highest call

up here in the sky
where crystals grow
where we are One
our seeds to sow

to cast the light
in different hues
across the world
unending views

Spring, he spins
he beams, he gleams
he flips, he sticks
effervescence seems

to flow up through
his legs that conceal
springs and energy
that his tricks reveal

For Zach x

The spring flowers
the autumn moon
summer breeze
winter snow

if useless things
do not clutter your mind
you have the best
days of your life

if you are lost, come
back to your breath
mental anguish
a quick death

you are loved
you always were
you always will be
may your mind be pure

wouldn't this be a
good way to be!

The shifting ghosts of
clouds in a moonlit sky
my heart bleeds, how had
I allowed my mind to cry

we all get lost in time
we all get lost in stuff
the stars bring us back in line
the night sky — simply enough

simply enough — I am gone
into stillness, that silent song
into the cold where all is clear
into emptiness, the full moon near

the moon it calls
for all to hear
come dance with me
come dance and cheer

forget your mind
we are one heart
we are one love
never to be apart

Oh hello there you
rainbow in the sky
your arch of beauty
within which I die

we are now together
in mind supreme
on this planet
in this dream

space time merged
the conscious stream
a dance in time
your beauty seen

time's purpose only
to experience this
existence, cyclic
temporary bliss

THE CONISTON MOUNTAINS
— HEATHER JAMES

The suggestions of light
the suggestions of form
from earth and nature
into our eyes borne

suggestions to entice
to draw us, our minds
into her way of seeing
capturing a slice in time

people existing in Aspatria
matter of fact, real
a mood ever changing
the weather full of zeal

Powerful energy
from head to toe
synched to the moon
synched to the glow

synched to the stars
synched to the sun
synched to all life
that has ever become

atone for it all
in this life and past
evil karma banished
devout, steadfast

humble and pure
the energy flows
let go and thrive
with the rose

the rational mind
blocks your gaze
being the light
end its days

turn it off
shut it away
wake up to infinity
and find the way

Great minds think alike!

the rational mind calculates
the still mind knows

use both in harmony...

Still your mind
and you will find
sublime energy
divine energy

the truth lives here
the remedy

There is a place
up in the sky
that is forever
souls do not die

connecting to this place
is our true path
a journey to take
to learn to laugh

but caution the road
is it littered with mines
ethics must harden
or the devil finds

ways to creep in
praying on the weak
impressionable, vulnerable
gullible as they seek

there is one simple rule
the route is monastic
monogamy at most
never listen to the plastic

looks are skin deep
vanity is sin
your soul's evolution
is a journey within

For Katya and Anne x

The work is good
the work is true
the shepherd works
with a grand view

up on the fell
down by the river
where life abounds
even if we shiver

the sheep are well
we are responsible for them
for their well-being
all does stem

they see with caution
they slowly trust
but always aware
that trust can rust

our job as shepherds
diligent and daily
checking on our sheep
helping those ailing

all the while
being with them here
in our hearts
where all is clear

The moon is full
the night is still
the sheep sit quietly
up on the hill

up on the hill
where all is grand
up on the hill
peace is at hand

a special peace
up on the hill
away from the chase
away from the kill

yet seeing all
with clarity, clear
if weather comes
our home is here

Skylarks, sunshine
still hill air
the glistening dome
across over there

Loadpot, your majesty
I do you salute
as I run your flanks
with awe, mute

silently you reveal
silently you shine
silently you sit
as I find my line

spring, in full flow
the skylarks call
oh to be here
now, with you all

you call and call
right to the top
I listen intently
and when I stop

you dance and play
on this spring day
beautiful iridescence
as I gently sway

A full moon in the east
the rising sun the same
may the wisdom you gift
forever remain

awaken to the east
as does the sun
a connected mind
in a heartbeat won

Allahu Akbar

The pull of el camino
drawing me in
a new world awaits
free of cluttering

For Juno x

Re-write the code
the code of your brain
whenever it panics
it is time to train

come back to the breath
feel your energy — roar
re-find your fearlessness
growl — open your core

let go of your thoughts
there is no wisdom here
come to the basics
rebalance and see clear

the light shows the way
the energy will flow
once you settle and shift
wisdom will then grow

Rivers flow
into the sea
burst your bubble
come home to me

when in tune
a river flows
dams get built
the pressure grows

pressure is growing
on our race
what will trigger
the wave of grace

sweeping aside
blocked minds
opening our passage
opening our blinds

seeing we are
a circle of One
the essence of life
evolved and become

inter-connected
kind and aware
nurturing our planet
with love and care

Lots of lambs about now!
some black some white
aah they lift our spirits
as the days become bright

the stirrings of spring
dancing all around
may you notice the moments
when its poetry abounds

enveloping and intoxicating
your senses and soul
oh for spring coming
delicate beauty, whole

How can you feel lonely
in a world full of life
it means you are not connected
your mind running rife

external gratification
will never fix this woe
the seeds of non-virtue
it will only sow

loneliness, the first symptom
of a mind getting sick
there is a way to fix it
which is gentle and slick

the way is to simply sit
and learn to meditate
it will settle your mind
and leave space to create

and in this spacious place
insights will click in
a growing awareness of love
a propensity for no sin

the Buddha's teaching is true
and the further you go
the small mind of loneliness
dissolves into a glorious glow

Rise above your intellect
shatter your mind's hold
your path and your future
wild, free and bold

divine energy to assimilate
in whatever is your way
feel it spread through you
a spacious place to play

synchronicity of happenings
as your life is revealed
a still mind of grace
the suffering healed

energy to read easily
love your best friend
space time collapsed
inside you, now bend

see that inside there is more
than you get from outside
the blinding light of truth
light that is your tide

see intellect as unnecessary
as the light holds it all
the singular truth beyond
where life is a ball

Buddi = intellect

The nature of creation
you can't learn it all
but you can know it inside
a swirling energy ball

and whatever pops out
from you is your job
to share and explain
to the masses, the mob

so connect, the light energy
inside you is existence
relax into the flow
without any resistance

all jobs are of service
to life and mankind
creativity is progress
let's all be aligned

There is an ancient language from
before the spoken word, a
language of the heart

a symphony, a dance, a poetry
between people, animals
and life not apart

the true nature of the universe –
The Way. Tao. Salvation from
the human condition

man's intellect is simply a tool of
existence and a necessary part of
life's evolution

Buddha nature can be found both above and below the intellect. I liken the intellect to a 'shit sandwich' – delicious on either side beautiful, serene, free of suffering

I had a traumatic brain haemorrhage in 2021. My intellect regularly malfunctioned in the course of my rehabilitation. So I found my way by simply letting go because I couldn't do anything else. I started sincerely offering myself to the universe in meditation and continue to daily. And everything slowly became beautiful. I gradually became aware of the higher energy connection in my centre and sought to maintain this 'centredness', a quiet mental state through my days. In between was beyond grim for myself and my family. I got neuro-overload whenever I found myself thinking much. So the only peaceful place to exist was in non-reaction, acceptance and humility. I set fire to my ego and out of the ashes a beautiful creature has arisen full of clarity, love, compassion, creativity and gratitude. ⟶

Trust the universe. There is a natural order. Let go completely and find your true part in it. This is the future of our species. Enlightenment. Your intellect will try to over-ride this by clinging to certainty it is constantly trying to manufacture. There is no 'proof' to this reality other than tasting the pudding.

Trust the universe. Trust providence. Trust the way. Enlightenment is simply a realisation of this. From this calm, empty state all arises. Divine energy manifesting into eureka moments, creative impulses and a clear code of conduct to live in harmony with all existence around you.

Deviating from this you will suffer mentally which can then manifest into loneliness and negative emotions such as greed, envy, hate, lust, desire, control. Unskillful behaviours which snowballs into arguments, fighting, wars. Equally stress and anxiety which then in turn leads to physical illness and/or mental illness.

Evolution is happening around you, no matter what you do. It is happening anyway. Why not join the party?

It's more beautiful than you can ever fully comprehend. A continuous flow of 'aah' moments. Intuitive ease. Peace. Mental clarity. Seeing behaviour for what it is. Seeing other people's auras and baggage. Knowing who you are and your job for humanity. Radiance. Mental and physical health. The proof is in the pudding.

You just have to let go and trust. But don't trust the charlatans! An enlightened mind has no self-interest. Just light and love.

The soft orange glow
of the moon rising
into the night-time sky
simply mesmerising

the settling energy
of a moon in wane
the chill still air
present, not a stain

heartfelt gratitude
a poem of love
I write this ode
from within, above

above in the sky
the energy alive
I feel it strong
my hand it drives

am I looking out
or looking within
who can tell
it's all beginning

to blur into Oneness
the stars and me
a place to know
called infinity

TOWARDS CATSTYE CAM
— HEATHER JAMES

The feathered hand of Thy embrace
honeyed by the wheel of time
I gaze upon this evening peach
in rapture of the moment seen

I lift and point — a skien of geese
travelling to a far off moon
as if it were within my reach
the tones of dusk — a waking dream

yet to touch am I
that which is within the sky
the boon of life that travels far
and points and says here we aar...

here we aar... You say anew
each day I rise and wake to You
I am here to record Your view
I am here to cherish, not rue

You pass across as Your light fades
my mind alight, creation made
the dancing threads alive and real
I tend to my sheep full of zeal

the air is crowned with Your gifts
which one to catch, that is Our rift
I am nothing, but a gift of yours
here to honour Your beautiful shores

Your lake that twists and stretches out
that hides within these oaks of old
Your lake that laughs when we are trite
that many have lost and won't be told

but the creation in us proves You are
within us, beyond us, beyond our minds
beyond our minds in a field of light
where all is spawned, that gives us sight

of sights to absorb and share with You
in this dimension of a worldly view
Catyste Cam, you call, I answer
I see you strut, you evening chancer

The way
is the way
sense it
at play
—
CIEL

Read the world
through your senses
making informed decisions
with clarity, not pensive

in a world sped up
survival of the fittest
still applies — is your
mind at its quickest

the only way to prevent
what's called oversaturation
is to empty and rest it
give it come ventilation

then when applied
it is laser sharp
with the right ethics
wisdom is a dart

so as we will see
mental health erode
those on the path
will find a peaceful abode

kindness, clarity
patient and love
the evolution of mind
as we head above

⟶

into a world of
fluidity and pace
where change is the wind
where the wind is grace

the epiphany of knowing
that the way exists
shows the path of humanity
the path that will persist

the purpose of my poems
of nature and beauty
is to sharpen my senses
and see that my duty

is to this planet
and equally our kind
so notice everything
your mind won't mind

don't judge or think
just give it a rest
then when it's needed
it will be at its best

Above two hundred is it you say?
I say union, alive, brave, free
waking up in the morning full of vim
if not, meditate and harden against sin

if separation comes, I am a mute labourer
— toiling in the 40° heat —
mouth parched, muscles aching,
mind at risk of racing

so I come to you, the energy of
my life, with all I am I listen
to your rhythm in my centre.
my mentor. my guru. my love

the love that showers the universe with life
the love that is shared by husband and wife
the love that flows through our hands
the growing strength of our young bands

a healthy heart is a fine thing
may yours be free of suffering
may the turmoil of the recent past be gone
may you craft sweet music all night long

beyond thought the music is here for all
the rhythm dancing through your body tall
the light that lifts your love above
that level you call connection

For Al x

Oh a billion shimmering stars
unfold within me
as I look out onto the vast expanse
glistening jewels of light — transfix
me as we float along

I stand in gratitude, the waves of
union lifting me to You
the energy of the morning light setting
off the honey in the air
sitting there silently, You listen, waiting
within spring's warming bark
the contrast of separation into harmony
— quite stark...

and so it flows
the river that grows
the torrent that swells
do I dwell?
do I hell!

I am here with you in the groves
I am here with you in the trees
I am here with you in the new leaves
come find me, it's you I chose
to join me in this life
to play with me in our garden
so come play with me
it's only you that does you pardon

Eruptions of colour!!!
the northern sky
oh may I be here
when I die

this place is nirvana
this place is heaven
the crisp morning light
the quiet time of seven

colour abounds everywhere
the crisp luminous green
the halo of white light
within which I teem

Live in your senses
not your thoughts

what more is there to say?!

—

CIEL

Live in your senses
not in your thoughts
whatever then happens
I can but pray

one thing is sure
eventually you will see
everything leads to unity

a jacket of faith
a cloak so vast
a wiping of suffering
from your past

a resetting of life
where harmony reigns
where beauty abounds
where only truth remains

when unity is lost
you will claw at its gates
let me in ! let me in!
I atone, please obliterate

any conduct that separates
any thought that permeates
from the devil and not the path
when unity is here
we relax and laugh

→

guided by the hand of God
the light of life, the path to trod
so I humble myself every day
I only ask you light the way

the way of peace
the way of unity
the way of the stars
the way of the sea

the way of the trees
the way the wind wends
the way of compassion
the way the mind bends

into the infinite, into the light
giving us peace, oh so bright

I am here. Now. Why is this
mystic poetry coming through this
hand?

To help aid unity!
To help people see!
To help them be free!

Free of the suffering of the
intellectual mind. To use this
tool as part of the role of mankind

We all have our purpose. With
a still mind we see. So still
yours now. Come home to unity!

I hear the songbirds
the songbirds of spring
the goldfinch, the wren
the wagtail within

the blackbird, the blue tit
the robin and sparrow
we are all one voice
merged and then narrow

the merging of voice
it can stay with us all day
the narrowing of the mind
checked by the way

the soft rain of night
has freshened today
the grass now growing
the birdsong here to stay

may you hear me sing loud
as I call and I call
may you come out of cloud
into the richness of all

enriched by the birdsong
enriched in your heart
enriched to be kind
as this day we start

The stars — they have drawn
                    me in once more...
no need for names in this state
this is the place from where we
come — from where we are — from
where we will go...

how can anyone get anything
done in this state — all I want
to do is dance and smile and
create. Nothing practical

an infinite state is this
bliss. Does my face show it?

all it wants is to experience,
yes a smile, but one lost in
an inner world of intoxication

the star within bursting out of
its bodily confine to join the
dance of the night-time sky

I am high, so high in this
moment of quiet peace

then snap. I am back. Life
calls — I get on with the washing up

SHARROW BAY AT SUNSET
— HEATHER JAMES

SHARROW BAY AT REST
— HEATHER JAMES

The lakeshore edge
at Sharrow Bay
something happened
I can not quite say

a moment, my first awareness
of a presence in me beyond
delighting in our surroundings
the shimmering lake — a wand

setting my core on fire
drawing me right in
to the movement, the dance
the lake surface — mesmerising

in this one special place
where all energies converge
womblike under the hills
as the waves gently surge

the rotation of the sun
Hallin Fell at twelve o'clock
the lapping of the waves
complete tranquillity — unlocked

my job is unequivocal
to bring this gift alive
to allow people to experience
what has helped me thrive

to then take back home
the work inside begun
of the magic that is Sharrow
in a heartbeat found and won

The Buddha he found deep
truth sitting under a tree
of how to live in peace
of how to be free

all of us are different
from different parts of the world
the truth it is the same
unifying, connecting, curled

curled into our core
that spacious place within
so wherever you live, whatever
your way, simply begin

my way is in nature
inner silence and in awe
a sitting practice daily
anywhere, on the floor

and then the truths they flow
the beauty it is revealed
of this sacred life we live
a world that is concealed

by the busyness of our brains
so stop it a while and see
we are all connected deeply
part of an infinite fruiting tree

The inner light
is my TV
I sit here quietly
in silent revelry

time is up-ended
it is free
to live this life
of simplicity

Find unity in
service to all

compassion for
One and all

All is One. One is all

One's true nature
working through me
One's true nature
the jackdaw, the tree

synching in nature
synching in form
acceptance and humility
in water borne

gifted with Samadhi
gifted with clarity
the life of One's mind
a life of charity

For Krish x

Delicate beauty
the primrose reveals
under the tree
in our field

keep going I say
the clouds they lift
the blueness comes
the jackdaws drift

in and out
building new nests
will yours stand
the strongest test

The Verse is here
alive in words
manifested, born
consciously heard

recorded in faith
reverence and respect
the Verse it flows
our duty to protect

life on the planet
interconnected, real
may the sun in these words
help you heal

Energy picked up
from a poem he wrote
two hundred years ago
distant, remote?

oh no I say!
read it and weep
for our brethren
our ancestors did keep

abusively, in bondage
Wordsworth saw true
abolition it came
but atonement was due

a legacy stained
by the unacknowledged
the time has come
I am astonished

by what atonement does
I am free, alive
for others well-being
I do strive

so look into your past
acknowledge wrong doing
hiding — a slow death
life needs reviewing

you will find peace
on the other side
a job for humanity
it's quite a ride

He crafts dead wood
into beauty and form
limbs without life
coaxed alive, re-born

the love there within
shared and the same
the eternal creator
shall always remain

For Steph ☺

THE PIKE OF BLISCO
— HEATHER JAMES

Drawing people from far
the Lake District heals
natural beauty in mountains
lakes, rivers and fields

the monastery of our land
since ancient times of old
the centre point, the core
the rugged landscape, bold

along its intricate paths
by its babbling streams
elevated views
clouds then light beams

deep into out core
getting into our bones
an upwelling of wellness
seasonal changing tones

a centre point for peace
come visit this land anew
walk out into wilderness
find your unending view

but always remember the gate
don't walk through unaware
my bull may be in the field
so take notice and take care!

Creeping under my skin
what is this itch
where did it come from
I listen to its pitch

its pitch is love
believe, it is true
love is all there is
the one true view

All that is left
is divine energy
it was my Nemesis
now my remedy

taking us beyond
to truth and love
taking us beyond
to divinity above

we are not supposed to know
how it all works
the mystery of creation
the mystery that lurks

inside every one of us
there is a guiding light
intuition, sixth sense
call it what you like

you only have to trust it
and your life will reveal
what was planned for you
just sit down or kneel

and allow the energy to circulate
through your body and mind
what some call emptiness
is actually mind refined

⟶

synched to the light
that has always existed
synched to the energy
of oneness that has persisted

since the dawn of mankind
since the dawn of strife
infinite and eternal
the seed of new life

the highest call is coming
for every living soul
the peace it exudes
will make us whole

but its work is never done
the cycle continues
the universe evolves
Yogis see its sinews

my job is here
in our sacred isle
the vanguard of progress
it has taken a while

to realise the significance
but Europe is home
the Lake District ancient
its most stately throne

The writing name CIEL is born out the phonetic sound of C-L, both my, Charles Lowther and my late mother Caroline (nee Ley)'s initials. In 2007, after my father's death, this is the name we came up with together, to embrace a new chapter of the Lowther family. Looking after people in a hospitality environment. We called our hospitality company CIEL Hotels.

The name then sat there quietly for the next 17 years until I had a spiritual experience that led to embracing the name and its significance both at work and as my writing name. We have since repositioned our branding at work to embrace this name, as opposed to marketing under a different banner.

The name was born equally from a female and male origin. It is not an English word, but a French word. Gender and race equality are at the root of CIEL's writings.

CIEL means the sky or heaven in French. We are all One.

There is no need for temples
no need for complicated philosophies
my brain and my heart are my temples
my philosophy is kindness.

—

The Dalai Lama

The seeds have now been planted
and so the fields are sown
the cusp of the growing season
ripe seeds wait to grow alone

encased in their hard shell
rain arrives to open the door
their roots will spread and link
the cycle continues once more

any seeds that don't germinate
will miss their time to grow
reabsorbed into the soil — a
life of light they will never know

A special thank you to Heather James, who has captured the Lake District's majesty with her artwork throughout this book. You can find more of her work on Instagram @rockpaperwateruk

Atop Helvellyn. Light streaming in as cloud cascades down.

The author. Standing still, welcoming the sun.